Write & Clean Farm

Om KIDZ
An imprint of Om Books International

Barn
Barn
Picker
Picker

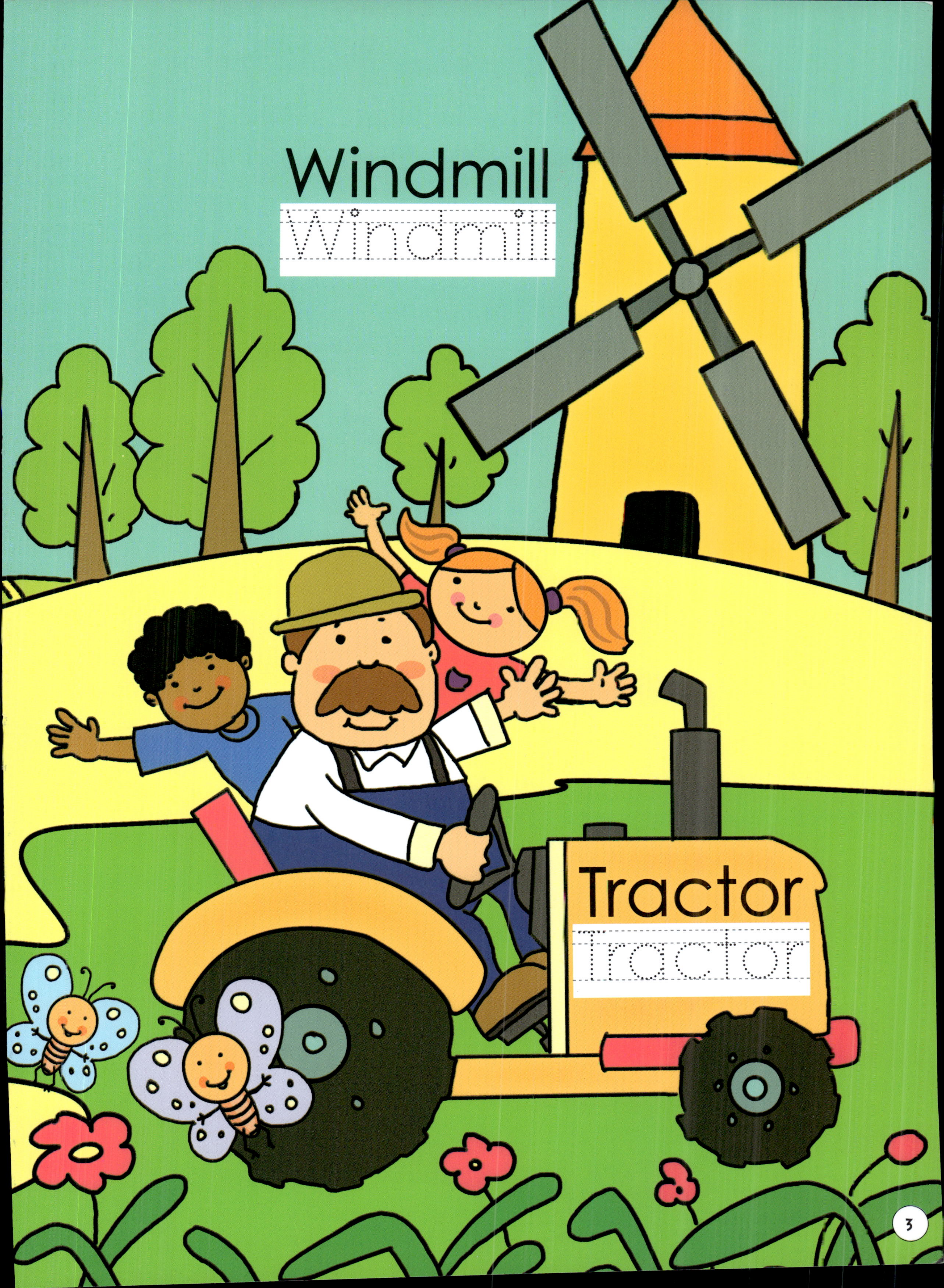
Windmill
Windmill
Tractor
Tractor

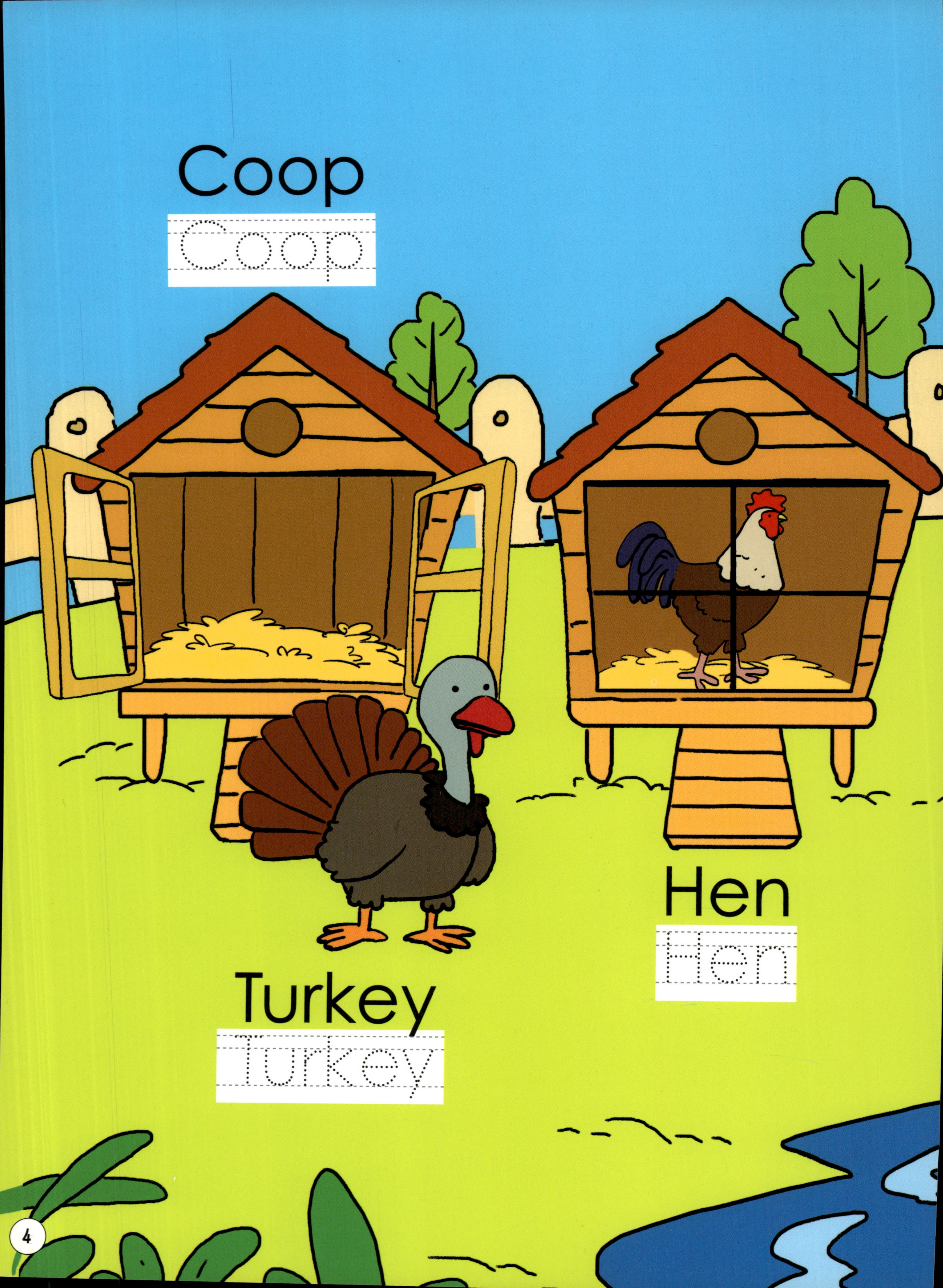
Coop
Coop
Turkey
Turkey
Hen
Hen

Duck
Duck
Pond
Pond

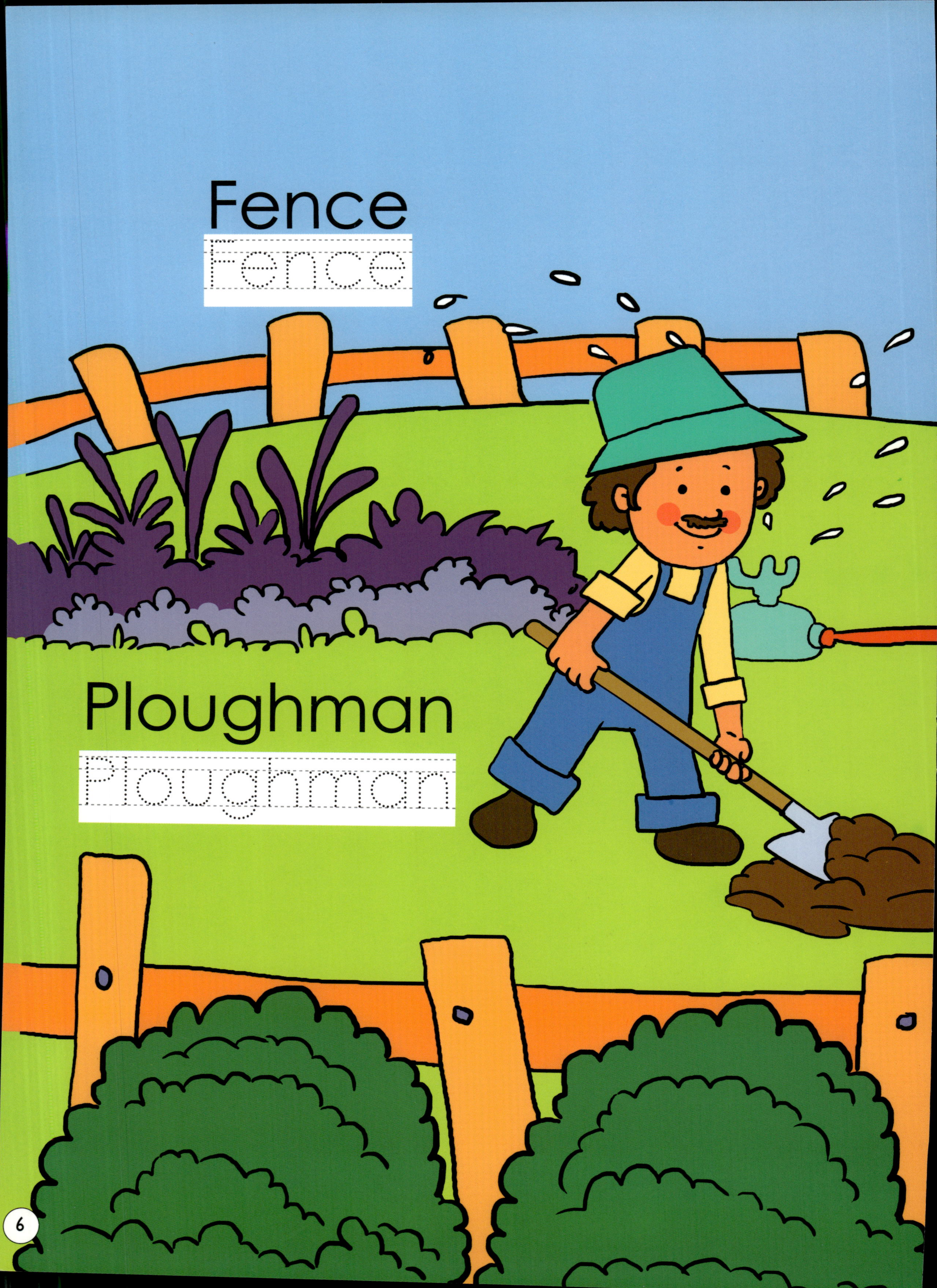

Fence

Fence

Ploughman

Ploughman

Shovel
Shovel
Garden Scissors
Garden Scissors

Straw
Straw
Barrels
Barrels

Farmer
Farmer
Grains
Grains

Chick
Chick
Cow
Cow

Horse
Horse
Dog
Dog

Sheep
Sheep
Milk
Milk

Hay
Hay
Eggs
Eggs

Write your favourite farm words.

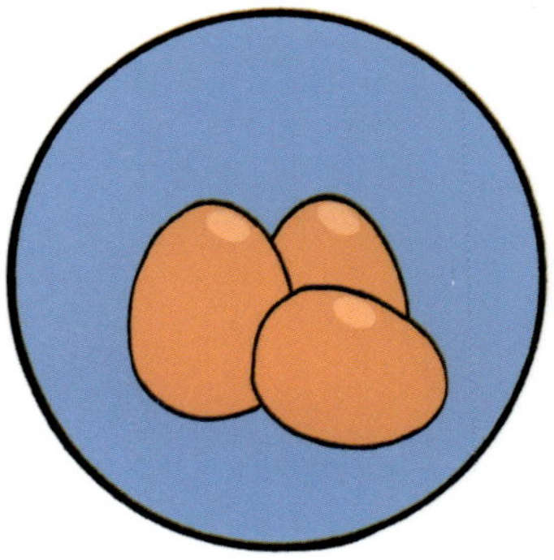

Join the dots and colour the animal.

Published in 2017 by

Om KIDZ
An imprint of Om Books International

Corporate & Editorial Office
A 12, Sector 64, Noida 201 301
Uttar Pradesh, India
Phone: +91 120 477 4100
Email: editorial@ombooks.com
Website: www.ombooksinternational.com

Sales Office
107, Ansari Road, Darya Ganj, New Delhi 110 002, India
Phone: +91 11 4000 9000
Fax: +91 11 2327 8091
Email: sales@ombooks.com
Website: www.ombooks.com

ISBN: 978-93-84625-29-0

Printed in India

10 9 8 7 6 5 4 3 2 1